YOUR
BONES

Sally Hewitt

This library edition published in 2016 by Quarto Library., an imprint of QEB Publishing, Inc.

6 Orchard, Lake Forest, CA 92630

© 2016 QEB Publishing,
Published by Quarto Library., an imprint of Quarto Publishing Group USA Inc.

Distributed in the United States and Canada by
Lerner Publisher Services
241 First Avenue North
Minneapolis, MN 55401 U.S.A.
www.lernerbooks.com

A CIP record for the book is available from the Library of Congress.

ISBN 978 1 60992 876 6

Printed in China

Publisher: Maxime Boucknooghe
Editorial Director: Victoria Garrard
Art Director: Miranda Snow
Series Editor: Claudia Martin
Series Designer: Bruce Marshall
Photographer: Michael Wicks
Illustrator: Chris Davidson
Consultant: Kristina Routh

Picture credits
t = top, b = bottom, c = center, l = left, r = right,
fc = front cover

Alamy 7 Jim Zuckerman, 21t Picture Partners
Corbis 13b Strauss/Curtis, 19t Virgo Productions, 19b Jennie Woodcock/Reflections Photolibrary
Getty Images 17t Barbara Peacock
Shutterstock fc S-F, 5t Teodor Ostojic, 5b Irina Klebanova, 6t Elena Elisseeva, 6b Alila Medical Media, 8 Roberto Kylio/Olga Lyubkina/Julian Rovagnati/Vitals, 9t Graca Victoria, 9c Dzm1try, 9b Kivrins Anatolijs, 10t Philip Lange, 10b Serghei Starus, 11b George P Choma, 12 Ariusz Nawrocki, 13tl Andresr, 13tc Gelpi, 13tr Kameel4u, 14b Cindy Minear, 15 Jiang Dao Hua, 21b JoLin

Words in **bold** can be found in the glossary on page 22.

Contents

Your skeleton

Your skeleton is a strong frame. It gives your body its **shape** and lets you move. It **protects** soft parts of your body, such as your heart.

Your skeleton is made up of **bones** of different shapes and sizes. **E**ach bone has a job to do.

Skull

Ribs

Backbone (spine)

Hip bones

Arm bones

Hand bones

Leg bones

Feet bones

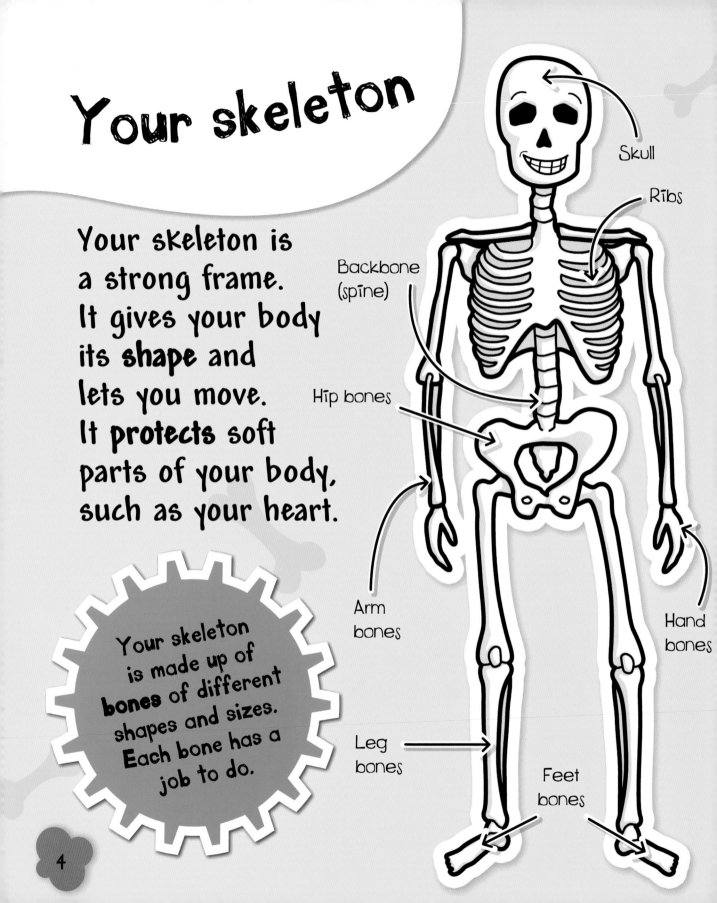

As you grow up, your bones grow too. Your bones also get harder as you get older. Some of them join together. When you are fully grown, you will have 206 bones.

A newborn baby has about 270 bones.

Activity

Which of your bones can you feel through your skin?

Can you feel the top of the bone in your upper arm? Your ribs?

Your bones

Your bones need to be strong and light. Bones are light enough to let you jump and strong enough not to break when you land.

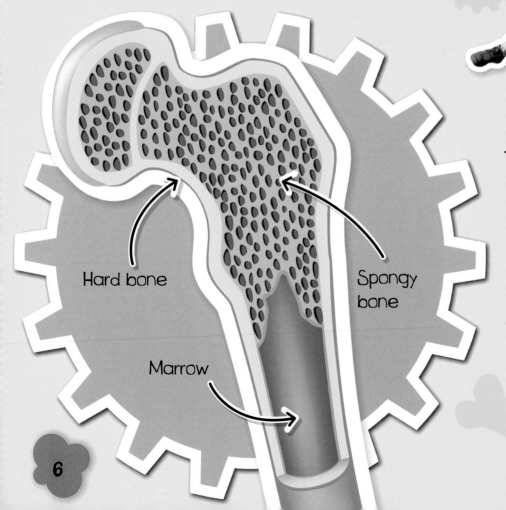

Hard bone

Spongy bone

Marrow

The outside of a bone is hard. The middle is like a sponge. Right in the center, many bones also have a jelly called marrow.

Even though bones are strong, they sometimes break. But bones are amazing! They can mend themselves and become just as strong again.

If you break your arm, a doctor **sets** your bone. Your arm is put in a plaster cast to hold the bone in place. Sometimes a sling is used to **support** your arm while it heals.

It usually takes about six weeks for a broken bone to mend.

Healthy bones

Just like the rest of your body, your bones need plenty of good food and **exercise**, as well as rest and sleep.

Calcium is very important for strong bones. Eggs, milk, and leafy green vegetables, also help to keep your bones healthy.

Do something active every day.

Exercise, such as running, dancing, or ball games, will help your bones to grow strong. What exercise do you enjoy doing?

You can have fun and look after your bones!

Wear a helmet when you ride a bicycle to protect your **skull**. Wear pads to protect your knees and elbows when you skate.

Joints

Your bones join together at places called **joints**. Most of the joints in your skeleton can move.

If you didn't have joints, you would be as stiff as a statue.

Activity

Move around. Which of your joints can move? What kind of movements can they make?

Your joints move in different ways. The joints where your arms join your shoulders and where your legs join your hips are called 'ball-and-socket' joints. These joints let your arms and legs move in a circle.

Ball-and-socket joint

Elbows and knees are hinge joints. They bend and straighten like the hinges on a door.

Your skull

Your skull is made up of several bones. It is very strong. Its most important job is to protect your brain.

Feel the shape of your skull. It has two holes for your eyes. Your jaw opens and closes when you talk and eat.

The top of your skull is exactly the right shape and size to cover your brain.

The bones in your skull give your face its shape. We all have a forehead, nose, mouth, and chin. Everyone looks different so we can recognize each other. It would be very confusing if we all looked exactly the same!

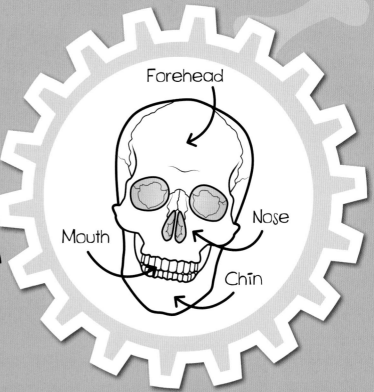

Forehead

Nose

Mouth

Chin

Activity

Look in the mirror and draw a picture of your face. Then draw your friend's face. Which parts of the drawings look similar and which look different?

Your backbone

Your backbone or "spine" runs down the middle of your back.

The spine is made up of 33 little bones. If it were one long bone, you would not be able to bend or twist.

Backbone (spine)

Activity

Bend over and touch your toes, then stand up again. Did you feel your backbone bend and straighten?

Your backbone holds you upright. Just like your skull protects your brain, your backbone protects the soft nerves inside it. These nerves carry messages from your brain to your body.

Gymnasts hold their backs straight to help them balance.

Your ribs

Your ribs are like a cage. They protect your heart, which pumps blood around your body, and your lungs, which you use for breathing.

You have 12 pairs of ribs. They are fixed to your backbone. The top 10 pairs of ribs are also fixed to your breastbone at the front.

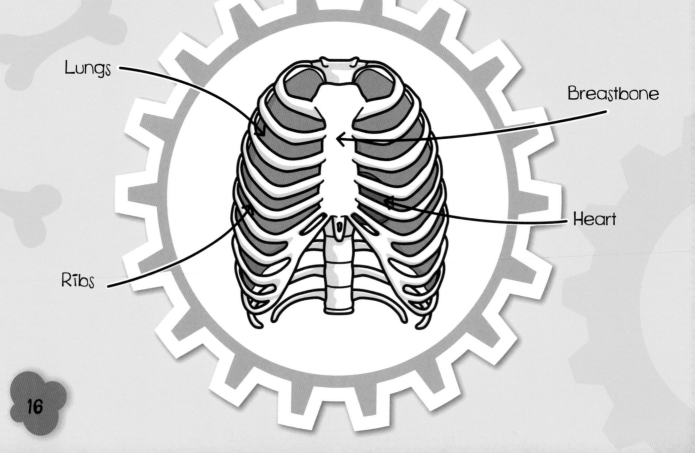

Lungs

Breastbone

Heart

Ribs

The bottom two pairs of ribs are only fixed at the back, so they can move easily when you breathe in and out.

You may be able to see the shape of your ribs through your skin.

Activity

You can feel your ribs move as your lungs fill with air. Put your hands on your ribs. Breathe in deeply. Feel your ribs lift and your chest get bigger.

◀ You have a special muscle under your lungs called the diaphragm. It helps to move air in and out.

17

Arms and hands

You use your arms and hands to grip and to pick things up, to write, and to play with toys!

Your arm, wrist, and hand make up 30 bones. These bones help you to make many different movements.

Elbow

Arm

Thumb

Finger

Wrist

Hand

The bone in your upper arm is thick and strong. You have two thinner bones in your lower arm and 27 bones in each hand and wrist!

Lots of little bones in your fingers help you make small movements.

Activity

Make a model with clay. Notice how you move all the bones in your arms and hands to make shapes.

Legs and feet

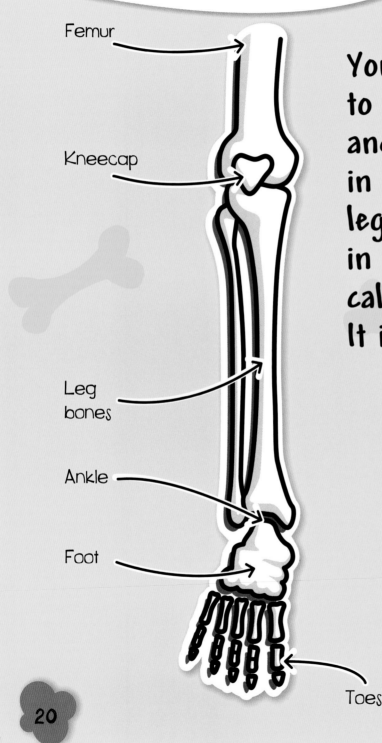

Femur

Kneecap

Leg bones

Ankle

Foot

Toes

You use your legs to walk, jump, stand, and sit. The bone in the top of your leg is the longest in your body. It is called the femur. It is very strong.

There are three bones in each of your toes – apart from the big toes, which have only two bones each.

A bone called the kneecap protects your knee joint. Children often bruise their knees, so kneecaps have an important job to do!

Have you ever cut or bruised your knee?

Activity

Put some dark paper in a tray and sprinkle flour on top. Stand barefoot in the flour.

Now step out without smudging the flour. Can you see how the bones in your feet spread out to help you stand?

You can see your footprints on a sandy beach too!

GLOSSARY

Bone

Bones are strong and light. The 206 bones in the body together make up the skeleton, which supports your body.

Calcium

Calcium is a mineral that is very important for healthy bones. Foods like milk, cheese, yogurt, nuts, and broccoli are rich in calcium.

Exercise

Exercise is moving around, for example running, swimming, jumping, stretching, and skipping. Exercise helps to keep your body strong and healthy.

Joint

"Joint" is the name given to a part of the body where two bones meet, such as your elbows or your knees. Most of your joints can move.

Protect

"Protect" means to keep something safe from being hurt. Your skull protects your brain.

Set

When a doctor sets a broken bone, he or she straightens it and puts it back in the right position.

Shape

Everything has a shape. For example, a ball is a round shape. Your skeleton gives your body its shape.

Skull

The bones of your head are called your "skull". They protect your brain.

Support

"Support" means to hold something upright or stop it from falling.

INDEX

NEXT STEPS

❄ Draw a skeleton with the children. Look at the picture on page 4 to help you. Talk about the shape of the bones as you draw them and feel them under your skin. When you have drawn the skeleton, stick it onto some card and cut it out. Now cut it into sections: head, body, arms, and legs. Put the sections back together using paper fasteners. Now your skeleton can move its head and limbs. Can you cut it further so that its knees and elbow joints move?

❄ Visit a museum with skeletons on display or look at a book with pictures of human, animal, or even dinosaur skeletons. Notice that they all have skulls and backbones. Discuss the differences in the shapes of the skeletons and the size of the bones. Why do some of the bones look different to ours? What could they be used for?

❄ Look at worms, slugs, and snails, which do not have internal skeletons to support them. Explain to the children that they are able to move without bones and joints.

❄ Talk about bones being strong and light. Look at different bones whenever you get the chance, for example, cooked chicken, fish, and lamb bones. Notice the differences between them and try to figure out which part of the body they come from. (It is best if the bones are handled only by an adult.)

❄ Ask the children to find all the places in their body that bend and help them name the joints. You could play a game of "Simon says", changing the instructions to: "Simon says bend your elbow (or wrist, knee, etc)." You must sit down if you bend the wrong joint!